THE

ART

OF

ART

THE

ART

OF

ART

Art is its Own Language

Dan Matson

Library of Congress Number: 00-190878
ISBN #:   Hardcover   0-7388-2073-3
                   Softcover   0-7388-2072-5

This work is a poetic statement about art.

This book was printed in the United States of America.

To order additional copies of this book, contact:
Xlibris Corporation
1-888-7-XLIBRIS
www.Xlibris.com
Orders@Xlibris.com

CONTENTS

*Art is its own
language*

*And poetry is
the voice of art.*

THEATRE

FOREWORD

Sight of sound,
sound of sight,

When did you cross
mind's programs

And sense that you
were not apart?

You did it
when intellect

Was approached
by art.

ART

OF

ART

I

ARTIST

Who enters art
satisfied

That all of it
is all of it?

*Seeing more
than before,*

*But less than
next encounter
will expose.*

Surprised by thought
that turns content
into form

That is to come,

Ecstatic when it arrives.

And art again
outstrips experience,

Which is delayed
by recognition,

Which waits for
acceptance

To recover.

While artist plunges
thru medium
so swiftly

that were revisit
not a fact,

What would be missed
would be missed.

*But art is not
that way.*

*For every action
there is reaction,*

*Though not equal
nor opposite.*

*For art reaches art
when notions scatter*

Along their ranges,

*Exhausting all possible
extremities,*

*And in the process
discover generations
of generations*

Of kindred

Emerging from
 unseemly sources
and directions.

Seeking identity
in disparity

That only art knows.

And energetic surge
quickens artist's pulse

As art strikes
repeated flashes,

And, briefly,

Only artist
holds original.

*And for unique
moment*

Is satisfied

*That all of it
is all of it.*

§

AESTHETIC

*What is the something
that makes something*

*The next something
of art?*

Note, stroke,
word, step,

Composition's
elemental bits

Joining, disjoining

*Conscious and
unconscious*

Thought and motion

*Arriving, leaving,
coinciding*

With random chance

Absorbing next
encounter

With choice.

What shifting strength
lies between

Deliberation's
casual effort

And steady pull
of gravity

That alternates
their clashes

And decides
into which clan
they are born?

*What is the meaning
of their meaning,*

*And when does
meaning*

Become art

That floats with fluid
sound of sight,
of thought, of move

Along creation's
flow,

Bumping, glancing,
swinging, stopping

Temporarily
here and there,

Until it finds
dimension's fit,

Catching, lodging,
staying, holding,

Fastening to
assembly's peers.

What ordains
fulfillment's moment

When attracted
universe

Of variables

Encounters unity's
composure?

*What lies beyond
composite's*

*Now distinctive
look*

Whose sequel
transforms future
into history,

As what was raw
becomes polished

To its brightest
glare of glitter

That sparks
attraction's burst

Upon aesthetic range.

Then having found
what all art finds,

When thermal peaks,
then cools, then melts

Into timely pools,

That its statements,
once their own
description,

Reflect their shine
no longer

*And lore and hype
sustain intimate
companion, sales,*

*Which thrive upon
an appetite*

Disdaining, forsaking,

Integrity's struggle,

While elements
maintain purity,

And position
to entertain
next spectacular

That holds
the value

That aligns
the something

That exceeds
the work,

And makes it art.

§

SPACE

*Space is inescapably
near.*

*Space is elusively
far.*

*What is space
that it surrounds
its surroundings,*

Near and far?

To define space
is to capture it

With just enough
form and color

To know in all
dimensions

It is there

And that somewhere
within the space
of space

Is spirit,

And neither spirit
nor space
show their trace

Except as art
reveals it.

Emerging art,
expiring art,

Growing, receding,

What is art
that it can
reproduce

The image
of space?

What is art
but mind's impression

Of the image
of the essence

Of the spirit
of the work

And the sense
of its mark.

For mark is more
than a mark

When it is made
with a sense

Than when it is made
without it.

And what else
remains

Of image
and essence

But the mark
of the spirit
of their art?

Is art a portrait
of what it portrays?

Or, being spiritual,
does it become
what it represents,

Even when it is
the space of space?

And space is
the perfect subject
for art,

As it evades
other description.

*And if art
can describe*

Anything of space,

*Can it describe
what is not
of space?*

Can art locate
spirit

When it leaves time?

Can it place
the place

Where it leaves space?

What? Does not
everything
reside in space?

Where then does
non-matter,
non-energy,
spirit, go,

When it elects
another universe,

When it is drawn
to the presence

Of that which made
both spirit and space?

Space, matter,
energy, spirit,

What will remain
of the essence
of their essence?

*Can art match
the cause*

Of what appears?

*Can it describe
its own founder?*

*Is appearance
the art of art*

*That describes
what makes it so?*

And, what is known
about it,

Is that nothing
can be shown

Without it.

For all in space
that art has shown,

Is there a side

That no time
and space

Have known?

*What is its sense
and its appearance,*

*And what is
its experience?*

What is that space,

Inescapably near
and elusively far?

Nothing,

Without its art.

§

CREATION

Worker works
familiar track.

Rhythm eases
random choices

Into what is there
and not there,

Detached from
other convention.

Consciously
unconscious

Of direction

That makes its way
restlessly,

Preferring style
above form.

*Rejecting structure's
tight constraints,*

*Neglecting
concentration's*

Studied charge.

*Unconcerned
where it goes,*

*Knowing only
it will know*

Arrival.

Stopping to look
and look again

For what is new.

And, having given
art its chance

To run past
boundaries,

Follows along.

*Driving farther
than before.*

*Losing control
to accident.*

*Perceiving flaw
as injury.*

*Resisting
recovery.*

For what emerges
from trauma

Is birth,
which is reason
for it all.

And more than birth,
uniqueness.

And it exists,
if not in fact,

Then in thought's
constructive mix,

Revealing encounter
in medium

More visible
than what is there.

For it shows
what it is

And says
what it is

At the same time.

And when it does
with feeling,

It is art.

And it colors
subject's object

For one to see
and other not,

While neither grasps
full intent

*That inspiration
contemplates*

*As a speck
or a universe,*

*While sensing
that all of art*

*Is but a speck
of galactic spark.*

And what is shown
is moment's share

Of what is known,

And what is left
is what is next

When art gets on.

And when it stays
for longer look,

Medium explodes,

And creation
proliferates

All of art,

And exposure
saturates

Every medium
with discovery,

*And, absorbed
with enlightenment,*

*Yields to further
stroke,*

And intensity
becomes emotion

Of pain and joy,

Merging with
satisfaction

That moment
did not expire

Before inspiration
was recorded.

And artist finds
the vision

That turns origin
to offspring,

And for awhile
is justified.

§

POETRY

What is seen
is not seen,

What is heard
is not heard,

Until knowing
becomes feeling

*That expression
has transposed*

*What describes
and what translates,*

*To speak them
to dependency.*

*For who can know
how well each
works,*

Or why they do,

*Till other senses
play with them?*

And playing sees

Perception feel

What sensing hears

Within the art.

*And excitement
enters spirit's place,*

*Where mergers
validate*

Arrivals.

*And, though unsure
of boundaries,*

Allows awareness

*Measured, shifting
definitions*

That poetry prescribes;

And having shown
artist its limits,

Offers other limits

Which are never
fully distinguished,

Or cluttered,

By reason.

And will not
interfere

When line is crossed
and recrossed,

For, in crossing,

Encounter rubs
enough edges

Until they fit.

But what puts
moment into play,

When, moment before,
thought eluded
all attempts

To add or subtract
from its sculpture

The stuff of all art,

Which causes artist
to skim all
surfaces,

Searching for
material

Relevant to form
and substance,

Without which
creation refuses
to emerge

From   oblivion,

And to show
its places

And be joined
forever

To its point in time.

And will not
be undone,

*For time has but
one direction*

*And cannot
reverse*

Or erase itself

And reject the work,

Though rejection

Is as much a part
of art

As endearment.

For the purpose
of art

Is to identify

Whatever is
of time and place

And to expect
response

As varied
as the art,

First, from artist,
then likely few,

Isolated by time
and distance

From all but
the art.

But affinity
claims its own

Who know, and see,
and hear, and feel

Because the art
is what it is,

Yet would be less

If poetry,
like the rest
of creation,

Did not still ask

How it comes to be.

§

MUSIC

Surface yields
familiar touch,

Feeling form's
innermost
instrument

Merge with player,

And touch is more
than touching

When soul joins
design

And knows
in an instant

Their sound is art.

Art of art,

Artist translates
every nuance

That transposes
waves' common forms

Into ecstasy.

And entertains
momentary response
to their birth,

Eager to hear
next release

Of progression's
fragments

*Of streaming flow
that one creates*

*And another
pronounces*

For others' tastes,

While absorbing
exposure's

Cumulative work,

Until it fits
its own niche

Of recognition.

*And sees what caught
the thought*

*That knew the theme
was not*

Of other work

When it rose,
floating,

From reservoir's
depths

To grasp venture
that lies before

What was never
heard before.

*Who has known
the mystery
of discovery*

*That artist feels
before sound
becomes sound?*

Which lingers
expectantly,

Riding waves

About to escape
mind's silent
conversion

Into sound
never to be stilled.

When does artist
release the work

And concede
reform's last chance,

Then stand the joy,
or remorse,
of time's reflection?

Who out there
will take it in

And surround
their time's events

With sound that claims

What otherwise
is forgotten?

*And who can number
the hearers*

*First touched by
popular intrusion,*

*Then by selection's
more stately
repertoire?*

What of independence
has music lost,
or gained,

When matched with words,

And each becomes
the other?

*And hearer takes
identity*

*From the feeling
both of them bring*

*As new music
immerses*

New self.

Music of music,
music of self,

That first is held
solely by rapture,

Then by rapture
and demand.

Music of music,

*What is music
that it begins
without sound,*

*And ends without
sound,*

*And would be nothing
without memory?*

And, for a moment,

Instrument places sound

Where memory
can reach it.

And player knows
that instrument

Accepts every mood
and every sense

That player brings,

And offers them
to music.

And music commingles
them as passion

For that which plays
closest to dream

Which touches all
in touch with
feeling

That surface yields

When its most
intimate touch

Invites its way
into art.

ʃ

SCULPTURE

Form pronounces
its entirety

Fully exposed,

Though must await
observer's

Less-dimensioned
grasp.

For who can view it
all at once

And verify
existence

Even with embracing touch,

Which does not begin
to feel the vision

and barely senses
the purpose

Of what it is.

And wants to ask:
Is its meaning
its design,

Or is something
missing,

Or left over?

*Must its being
mean something?*

*Is mass not equal
to its look?*

But what choices
brought it

To what it is,

Whether or not
it was meant

To be that way?

For how exact
was the measure

Of the mixture
of intent
and accident

From origin
to final touch?

And which was its
true birth:

When concept flashed,

Or when decision
clashed

With indecision?

*And resolved
that, either way,*

Form is formed

*By addition
or subtraction.*

And knew the space
it would displace

And if its parts
would be moving
or rigid.

And kept asking,

By what process
it became art,

And if a thing
to be worshipped?

*Was it when shape
matched creator's
vision?*

Which vision?

*Why from countless
rejects*

Did this one stick?

Motioning thought

Into labor's
intense construct,

Seeing, working,
working, seeing

Collective being

*Resisting stretching
intuition*

*Farther than
it cares to go.*

Momentum slowing,
ceasing, locking,

Avoiding one last

Step too far.

*Imagination's
reality*

*Now fully
punctured.*

*Proposing
what it knows*

By what it shows.

Finished statement
stilling artist's

Frenzied desire
to be felt

By some viewer's
racing heart.

Now satisfied
by any response
to the object,

Which itself owes
existence
to reaction

To what was there
and not there.

*And hides nothing
that insight's look*

Will not reveal,

*Once viewer
discovers*

*The final form
of art.*

§

ART

OF

ART

II

II

THEATRE
(PROLOGUE)

Sight of sound,
sound of sight,

When did you cross
mind's programs

And sense that you
were not apart?

You did it
when intellect

Was approached
by art.

THEATRE

Day slips into
other garments,

Lights dim, doors close
at divergent points

And streams converge
at the confluence

Of art's monument,

Before the sight
of sound arrives.

Funneled masses
filter thru observers
of other things to do,

And rush to stake their places,
reserved next to exciting,
unchosen others

Whose random glances
capture attention

In subtle ways.

Cavernous space
contains within

Its still quarters
yet to be lit,

Murmurs nearly
inaudible;

Dark, dark sound,
absent rhythm

And without tone
to usurp the mind.

Last chance for thinker
to think alone

And pause to let
sensual drought

Seep through ruffled
expectations

Of production's
strengths and flaws.

Soothing respite
from billings' draws

Which soon enough
begin their play,

For here architect
has consigned silence

To intruder's role.

And, in transition,
sound will pause

And turn to tune
its tuning,

And await first
advent of beat

Which, from downstroke,
dictates all to come

From vocal source
and counterparts

Now holding polished
cords and chords.

Labyrinth cave
is awakening

As it beholds
viewers' world

Which meets to mix
its sound with light;

And, as appointed,
it commences.

Players play and
viewers view;

One thinks what
other does

To see what plays
in other's dreams,

In one titanic
consolidation.

*Sealing inside in
and outside out,*

*Confining the
experience*

*To the viewers
and the players,*

*For the doers
are the payers.*

Not allowing art to escape
beyond prescribed space

Into grasp
of unlicensed artifice,

Nor its notes and measures
diffuse for outsiders'
reference to generic sound,

Without presence
of acoustic delight.

Ah, but inside,
the thing thrives upon
its generated imagination.

Emotional mix
its own leaven
for sum of the parts,

Rising beyond
representative assembly.

And there is no   unravelling
nor sorting out,

For without all of it
there is no value

Past the slightest spark
of a note.

Is performance all
that its about?

Or is it more that
life's compositions

Bring audience
to this point
of diversion,

Or even less,
to the one

Individual

Person,

Me.

So, should I sit
and take it in?

And edge and move
with quiet breath

On whisper of
commentary

Acquired from
program's print,

Which only speaks
in broadest terms

Of artist's plan?

And know, performer
brings to each work

What audience brings
from its work.

Seen that way,
the whole thing

Is less glamorous
than it would be,

But on its own level
is glamorous

And the thing to do.

Now does the sight
of sound flow out

To gala rows
of human waves,

Replacing noise
which woke up day

And cluttered its
entirety.

Superior force
of structured symbols

Floats far away
the pain of thought

As it immerses
in medium

Weightier than atmosphere's
less cerebral fluid.

Until distress
of foremost care

Cascades down
deepest chasm

Which distances
purveyor from enthralled,

To lie submerged
in bottomless pool.

While above, both may
reach across

Interpretive bridge
toward other's response,

And not till later
do any reflect upon

What drew them here
to confront the art,

The artist, and self.

Then well along
performance path

Resistance to
enchantment wanes,

And edge no longer
rubs and grates

On eye and ear.

But each absorbs

Until neither
keeps to itself

What seemed to be
exclusive claim,

Before the sight
of sound arrived.

And mesmerized
by swinging chain
of highs and lows

Flowing with ecstatic crests,

Then dropping off
monotonous rolls,

Focus turns its look
to neighbor

Now counting scenes
to build an act,

Then another
and another,

Hoping that impatience
is anticipation's way

To end time's captivity.

Then climactic tremble
surges in higher waves,

Pushing out
in the only direction
it knows

Until monument shakes
at every pillared wall,

Where waves pile up
without escape

From reverberation's beating.

Where can medium
go from here?

It is enough.

Artist offers no more
beyond symbol

Riding flow of final wave

Greater than the rest,
which, for brief moment,

Inundates hall
from ceiling to floor

Wall to wall,

Ear to ear.

And finally convulses,

Pressing passions
to their seats

Before accord releases
reimbursement,

Lunging to its feet,

Throwing back
latent inhibitions

So long stored.

*Now sound and sight
unite,*

*Calling curtain's
repeated flight.*

And structure collapses.

Discipline subsides
into disarray,

Pouring waves
of new energy

Into the night,

To go inspired
to its own bed,

Where it tunes out
deliberation.

And dreams translate
what senses felt

After the sight
of sound arrived.

§§

POSTLOGUE

Sight of sound,
sound of sight,

When did you cross
mind's programs

And sense that you
were not apart?

You did it
when intellect

Was approached
by art.

§§

COMPOSER
(PROLOGUE)

What ear first felt
wave's tingling notes;

Sense absorbing,
voice reflecting
unrestrainable expression,

Joining endless chords,

And what mind first
composed their symbols,

Translating, transmitting

Common language
of the stars?

And who first meant
to hear it

With the spirit?

COMPOSER

Who dreams of sound
not yet composed

And not played out
on instrument

Known to man
or nature?

Who would dream that?

Whoever believes
that nothing

Has reached
its limits.

Sound of sound,

Energy breaks
with matter

Only to rejoin
in ebb and flow
of wave

Expending indelibly
in mind's recesses.

Solo sound,
crowded sound,

Strung in line,
wrapped in chord,

Filling its only
point in time,

Then floating off
to join the noise

Great sphere makes,

Passing its place
in space.

One plays a note,

Note makes a sound,

Rounding each ear
of audience.

All receiving
waves of tones

With no two thoughts
of them alike.

Differing by
each hearer's likes
and dislikes

Wrought from moods
surrounding

Their arrangement
and performance,

Meaning nothing
to what is art,

Only to what
is thought of art.

Emotion's entry
giving meaning

Without reason
readily known

Except to one
who cares to hear

What artist said.

Who knows if sound,
beyond all words,

Means nothing?

And what is "thought"
to take meaning

From what is heard
and not heard?

What is "thought"

But that it comes
in collections

Of senses' works

Brought together
by the physical

To mind's translator

And used or stored
for life's demands.

Or that it
originates

Somewhere inside
interior
of innermost
responder,

Which joins itself
first to what
it knows well,

Then to less
familiar types

*And holds for final
transformation,*

*When its most
permanent parts*

*Are gathered to the
spirit that claims them.*

*Which sounds will
it select*

*As it assembles
for timeless state?*

Composer, did you
consider that ?

Sound without waves,
without transmission,

Without volume
to adjust,

For spirit needs none
of it.

*When uncertain
artist questions*

*Whether doing
is worthwhile*

*In those lonely,
bewildering,
creative times*

*And still lonelier
times that follow*

*When only artist
knows their meaning*

And, dreaming dreams,
hopes that work

Is successor
to the person,

Even if just to
next generation,

Which may by chance,
or even reason,

Finds in the art
some element

Of truth that lasts.

How shortsighted.

Where is value
in the doing

For sake alone?

Should not artist
be gatherer

From production's
finest encores

To add to store
of unfathomed

Thrills of hearing

Favored sound
to take along

Past life's journey
to forever,

When sound no more
is only sound
of sound.

§§

DANCER
(PROLOGUE)

Art moves artist
to become art.

Art leads
artist follows.

Where do they go?

To anywhere

That escapes
their world

And finds another.

*And reaching it
will only be*

*When art moves
artist
to become art.*

DANCER

Rhythm stretches mind
beyond thought,

Pulling its partners
past their places,

Dancing all
its programs.

Twirling forms
spilling sparkling
particles

Thru swirling clouds,
stirring their spaces.

Light glances
from each
reflecting limb

As senses
collaborate

To join their art.

Awakening thought,

*Transforming dreams'
unconscious effort,*

*Aware of motion
only when it ceases.*

Image transits
performance'
fluid form,

Confirming the span

Where art begins
and ends.

Flowing, sweeping,
within range
of all who ask

Which side of art
they have indulged,

Before they embrace.

And artist,
not content
to view the art,

Must be in the art
to feel the art.

Taking risk
of consequence

Of what is art
and what is not.

Not fully yielding
to what purports

To make it art.

And art, confident
of itself,

And knowing its own
spectacle,

Is indebted
more to artist

Than to critic.

*Trusting intuition's
instinct*

That thrusts the soul

*Beyond last familiar
encounter*

To the place
where creation

Transforms excitement
into art,

And continues
to thrive

While the luxury
survives.

And creation knows
each step

At its own
sequential birth,

When it first appears
without rehearsal.

And recognition
seizes memory,

Insisting it record
its art

Before fleeting claim
is lost

To oblivion.

And moment flies,
lifting lightly

All within it,

On a way
not entirely

Theirs to resist.

Senses caught
catching senses

Carrying ecstasy
further aloft,

Leaving below
all that distracts
and detracts.

How high art rises
on senses' wings,

Hovering, breathing
rare exhilaration,

Unconcerned by
destiny's

Destination.

Knowing only
it has arrived,

When art moves
artist

To become art.

§§

ARCHITECTURE
(PROLOGUE)

*Architecture is
the art*

*That surrounds
with art*

*What it builds
with art.*

ARCHITECTURE

Mass intrudes space,
imposing shape,

Settling view
for more than one
generation.

While earth is marked,
imperceptibly,

By contours seeded
on fortune's winds,

Not measuring time
by lifespans.

Undisturbed,
unperturbed

By extra-natural
creation

When encroachment
is still distant

And not yet
a neighbor

Who waits to see
the final plan,

Not always matching
end result.

And, when in place,
is committed
irrevocably

to being there,

With choices made
for voices raised

But not heard.

And art remains
until elements'
transforming touch

Plays wearing games
with what was once

Perceived in awe
as permanent.

*And aesthetic's
hallowed, untiring
look,*

*Marked history's
value of the age.*

Then, after all
preserving means,

Time itself declared
extinction
of the craft,

To be followed
by the art.

*And land again
vegetates*

*As culture leaves
or disappears,*

*And history questions
existence*

Until successor plan
grasps boundaries,

And even more intense
formula

Projects design
which overwhelms
all memory

By magnitude
of latest dream

That technology
enlightens,

Which brings new art
to what is thought
possible,

Until it is.

Monumental
monument

To social age,

Reaching higher,
collecting more
of everything

To put within it

Especially
what is new.

And theme attracts
content,

And content theme,

Illuminating day
with protruding gleam

of new art.

And the night
by internal glare

That signals where

Occupants spend
its utility.

And where each
marks ownership

Amidst the art
each places

To show where
each belongs,

While structure
tolerates it all.

Just as building
by its statement

Seeks acceptance
in diversity,

And needs not beg
to be observed

For what it is.

*Nor does next
distinct intrusion*

*That contrasts
with what is there,*

For it is there.

And what is next
would not become
what it will

If architecture
was not the art

that brings it
to reality.

Architecture
is the art

That surrounds
with art

What it builds
with art.

And resolves
to settle designs
on nature

And whoever else
has a view

when it arrives.

§§

AUTHOR

Scanner floats
on whirling planes,

Searching memory's
swirling contours

For bits to fit

Words descriptive break
with encounter.

Probing moment
long enough

To dilute mind's
myriad clots,

Pouring thoughts
into fissure.

Until gap
is filled and sealed.

And, relieved,
turns to next
inquiry.

Hoping query
matches theory

That precipitates
another split

Of space from matter,

And redefines
the edge of art.

Adding more myriads
of myriads

To multiples
of multiples

Of records
of records

Of thoughts
of thoughts

Which, as with
all of art,

Begin with one,

That waits
to be said

In the way
art speaks

Through drafter
who needs to say

That identity
of the saying

Is the spirit
of the sayer.

Hoping to be
understood

While attempting
to understand

What seeing sees
and hearing hears.

Documenting,
capturing,

What it will,
when it will,

For recall wants

What it will,
when it will.

And then turns
to retrospect,

And pauses
to examine

What it is,

Rather than what
it seemed to be

*And the pleasure
that satisfied*

*What moment held
most important,*

*Until retold
with other*

Satisfaction.

Conceding

How much better
the successor

That holds its place,

Not to be discarded
like its forbears.

Enjoyed enough
to be seen
again,

And be lifted
by the curious
and the familiar

From volumes
of volumes

*In circulation's
flow,*

*And kept afloat
on the surface*

*Of accumulation's
deep, anonymous
storage.*

*In what buoyant
clanging wrapper*

*Must its content
appear,*

*To attract
media's glaring
flash?*

Why must art
be campaigned

By other art

For its own
survival?

Inextricably
linked

To prized awards,

Heralding
its glorious,

Best-selling
self.

As creator's name
edges past
mortality,

And the value
of the work.

*Counting next
publication's run,*

And the next,

*As promotion promotes
its promoter.*

And scanner,
still searching
for art,

Finds it broaching,
plunging, reaching,

To grasp its
author's hand.

§§

FILM THAT MOVES

Story breaks
from silent frames

More than once
upon the time
that time gave it.

Reviving revival
before it slips
archival worth.

And while silence
shouts at story

Time lives again.

Moving beyond itself
without losing its place,

Recapturing reality
in all its dreams.

*Having once altered
their alterable state*

*And made space
irrelevant,*

Except for viewer's view,

*Whose space, like time,
need not be.*

Like actors acting
outside the real.

But that is real acting,

Just as performance
is the art
that has designs

On time and space,

And holds its own
with both of them.

What is this art
that it exists
of itself,

And illuminates life
in darkened rooms

Where emotions surge,
unabashed by light.

Finding the same
cover

That life seeks.

And reality stages

Every novel departure
from its norms,

Until they project
other norms,

Edging uncommon tale
into common lore.

That informs
a generation

Of its every crisis
and solution.

Reaching, stretching
self-fulfilling

Resolution.

And in the process
manages

To entertain.

And draws comment

Until commentary
is the entertainment.

*And figures face
familiar screen,*

*Filling all familiar
roles.*

*Wondering how well
audience reads them,
and fills its roles,*

Responsively or not.

And for how long.

*As each frame rides
exposure's path*

*Revealing art's final
movement*

Then reels away.

*While memory flickers
at one last flick.*

§§

ART

OF

ART

III

III

PHOTO

Time leaves senses
and their faces

Looking back
to what exposed them,

When neither
are around.

*Marking moment's
past and future,*

*Inviting memory
to compare them.*

Knowing they
will not repeat,

Despite desire's
strongest urging

To redefine
reminiscence.

*Stretching question's
widest reach*

*From way it was
to way it is.*

What is there now
but memory?

Has sense reflected
long enough

To confirm
what it perceives?

And is not sense
not singular?

Does not one sense
stimulate

Memory
for another,

Ensuring its find?

Who is image for,

*That it excites
enough interest*

For second look?

Could it be
because of who

Is in place
and who is not,

And who is with
whom?

And one delights
while other abhors

The same vision,

However they reflect
the circumstance
and age

That taker took.

And what was left
that aim excluded

From its tidy range

Is gone forever.

*Which is the same
forever*

That image faces,

*For as long
as it lasts.*

And if the art of it

*Is the art
that captures
and preserves,*

*What is its
duration worth?*

Impression's best,

What appeal
invites comparison

With you

And the real thing?

Is it your lack
of abstraction

That recognition
serves?

That identifies you
without effort

And interprets
whatever art

Allows is less
of form

Than substance?

*How technical
is the eye
of art?*

*And where does art
depart from
science?*

Or do they both
reside within

The chemistry

Of their offspring?

What is experience,

That it deserves
to be disturbed

By recollection

That excites memory
to perform

Beyond its norm,

And beyond
its choice?

Slender slip
of evidence

That turns the eye
that sees the look

Within the page
that bares the past.

You are a sight.

§§§

CYBERSPACE
CYBERSOUND

What is the space
of cyberspace

And what is the space
of spirit?

Is all of space
in one space,

Or is some of it
just near it?

Plus, minus, plus,

Object shifting
into subject,

Form forming form

With or without
space.

Pulse, impulse, pulse,

Membrane bending,
throbbing, sending,

Transcending
antiquity's plain
and jungle.

Plus, minus, plus,

Tracking, running,
energy's paths;

Sensing, pacing,

Atmospheric
cyberspacing.

Pulse, impulse, pulse,

Old sound pounding,
cadence counting

Universal beat,

Greeting new
vibrato.

What becomes
of drums

And orchestral kin

Pressed within
electronic board

Or searching spin
of floating disc

Concealed from all
but theory?

Does spirit beat
within them still?

Equation's form
transforming form,

Linking waves
to panel's print,

Shrinking time
and distance

*As it extracts
craft from art,*

*Tolerating loss
of substance,*

*Judging process more
by what it is not*

Than what it is.

Plus, minus, plus,

Percussion's wind,
cymbal's string,

Artisan's art
now synthetic
syntheses.

*Phrases of
paraphrase,*

What art is left?

*What aesthetic
can logic know
beyond itself?*

Space without space,

Reality rearranged
in circuitry.

Testing structure
less for coherence

Than for randomness.

Plus, minus, plus,

*Particles flash
momentary look*

*Past recognition's
screen,*

*All seeming
not to collide.*

Pursuing energy's
great magnet

As direction slips
its smaller orbits

Pulled past feeble
random range,

Riding instant
lifetime.

Plus, minus, plus,

Fuzzy logic
living between
the spaces

Where intuition's
sensors lie,

While spirit clears
next clearing.

Pushing, pulling,
engaging, refining

Its etiquette,

As inertia's
motion

Feeds upon itself,

Keeping intact
what sets it off.

*Since what matters
to matter*

*By energy's
compulsory turn,*

*Is avoidance
of other matter,*

*For when direction
straightens,*

*A target
gets in the way.*

Except in cyberspace

*Where the logic
of equation*

*Transforms matter to
perception*

*And x and y
and yes and no*

Are equal art.

*Must musician be
mathematician?*

*Who else can
place the place*

*Where theory's wave
crosses space,*

*And get it there
intact,*

*To hear it
interact.*

Plus, minus, plus
pulse, impulse, pulse,

How near and timeless
can sound's wave be,

Bringing more life
to being

Than what describes
of what exists

*Which first had heard
that, unlike space,*

*Time has less
to go around,*

*And found convenient
way*

To double up.

What is the sound
of cybersound

And what is the sound
of spirit?

Is all of sound
of one sound,

Or will some of it
just hear it?

§§§

CYCLE

What artist, having
strung production

To its endless
seeming end,

Has not encountered
that end,

At least once.

And, having been there
more than once,

Knows, too, that end
will reach its end

When it will,

While work pauses
until it does.

And, at propitious time,
waiting ends,

Anticipating
what is next,

As interlude
clears view

For what is new.

And time slackens
constricting hold

On notion's offspring
lodged in enclave's
mental alcove,

And thought floats free.

But, until then,
doubt squeezing doubt

Denies that art
is cyclical

And must rebound
from nether world.

Instead it drags
valley's bottom

Ever deeper,
not finding it

And therefore
does not release
anxiety

From realization
that irretrievable
time is lost,

And with it
what number

Of works not born.

And just as heights
spiral upward

At each giddy
completion,

As each work feeds
upon the last,

So is alliance
of drought
with gravity

Which needs nothing
to aid descent.

So down it goes,
deeper than place

Where anticipation's bubble
has ever burst,

Or recognition
has ever stared.

What can penetrate
gloom so dark

That it excludes
all color of light.

While load weighs
heavier

Than mind can ever fathom
or acknowledge.

Crushing compress,
too dense to squirm
away from,

Heaping, pressing,
straining, stressing,

Collapsing
into futility

Where no appeal
to chance remains.

Final thought
of mariner
and sub-mariner

Whose deepest intrusion
condenses conclusion.

Is there still hope
for creator?

But what does
creation imply

If not struggle
with nature's odds

And all that mind
perceives of it,

Especially beyond
what is known.

What use is art
if it does not reach
the unknown?

And nature,
finding no threat,

Acquiesces.

Remembering,
understanding,

It was creation
that produced it

And brought it to
survival's edge,
and keeps it there.

And sensing artist
may be proper
companion,

And, even more,
an ally,

And hastening
to assist,

Breaks its own law
as it has
at selective times,

And releases artist.

Was it really
nature's bondage

That relinquished hold?

What can nature
do of its own

To spirit that moves
within it?

Is it nature
that doubts value
of the work?

Transposing doubt
from value of art
to value of soul

Which, even
occasionally,

Doubts its own mate,

Spirit.

And, forgetting past,
sees only self

In hiatus.

And may question
how to compose
what it did before

Without recalling
how to do it.

Silly,

What was done
will not be done
again.

Why should artist
even want to ?

For creation
happens only once,

After that it is
something else.

*And even fear
of doing
or not doing*

Is rejected,

*And with it
fear of doubt,*

*And their control
of hand and eye.*

And the silence
of creation

Overwhelms
all thought,

And is the loudest
sound
mind will know,

For nothing else
can be heard.

And enterprising art,

*Having again spent
tribute's dues,*

*Restarts its long
assembly line.*

§§§

CRITIC

*Any person
knows better
than other person*

*What artist
does with art.*

*And can pronounce
the art of art*

*That claims
or rejects*

*Other's likes
and dislikes*

Even without
being there

To enjoy
the agony

That nature feels
when artist takes

Another view
of what is there.

And turns it
first into self,

Then into art,

For nature to see

Before the light
is gone.

*What then does
singular mind*

Comprehend of art

*That thinks it
will translate*

*All that art
would have it say?*

Can an affair
with art

Ever allow
perception

To enter, and leave,
perceiver

Without prejudice?

How well can
intermediary

Align senses'
intimate rapport

With those of artist?

What is the worth
of trying

To speak of that

When art is there
to present itself?

And when time
adds other views,

How many times
does comment
reconsider,

Or reverse,

While art remains
unperturbed?

*Since when does stature
of comment rise*

To merge with art?

*If art will not
participate,*

Why should artist?

How much of art
is creator's intent

And how much
is accident

That sends design's
shifting motion

In undesigned
directions?

As unforeseen
as commentator's
own view

That life thrusts
into the same wind,

Until it drifts
and settles,

Hardly selecting
place or meaning.

Must there be place
or meaning

To belong?

Is not art
life's stimulus

That requires nothing
but to be known
as its own?

*Though art is brought
to dwell somewhere,*

*Where time is spent
with companion,*

Memory.

What then is observed
of art

That is not revealed
by art

To add to life's
experience?

Does it matter
that all of art

Is just some of art
until more of art

Appears?

*To be called
by art*

*To ignore
detractors' cries*

*That take issue
with everything*

That art accepts.

And somehow think
issue causes issue
to be art,

When it is art
that orders issue
to be noticed,

And takes issue
only with
pretender

Whose purest truth
is far from where
the soul is,

And speaks with words
of words

That show nothing
of the art.

While everyone
but critic
knows that

Art is its own
language.

§§§

AWARD

What is art for,

*That it excites
creation's urge,*

*While distraction
trims*

Its closest edge?

*And holds focus
for a moment*

*Until moment
overwhelms*

Memory.

*How enduring
is art of art*

*That first draws
attention*

To glitter's gaze,

*Then later
attaches reason
to its notice.*

And expends all
its energy

In frenzied search
for likely place

To be seen
or heard

Outside itself.

*Is art its own
rival?*

Is the purpose of art

To be,

Or to compete?

*As it crosses
compulsion's line*

*That divides
creation*

From promotion.

*Or does motive
belong to both?*

Art of art,

That forces risk
to abandon

What makes you new.

Your companion,

*Whose commerce
is barely art,*

*Knows nothing
of experiment*

*That thrills each
discovery*

To another.

And is content
to remain

Where acclaim gives
aid and comfort

Without knowing
its detractors

And the prospect
that attracts

Next breakthrough,

And soon forgets
what got it there,

And succumbs
to expectations

Of great reward

*From copies
of copies*

*Of pieces
of pieces*

Of artist's work.

And drive
is driven

To drivel,

As essence
evaporates

From original.

And with it
the line
that is not a line,

That discerns
what is art

And what is not.

That knows it
when it sees it.

*And questions
enough
of what it is*

*To ask
if what it is*

Is what it is

And not the noise
that surrounds it.

For art is art

Only in contrast
with what exists.

*And will be reserved
for a time,*

*While expectation
divorces*

Recognition

From the charade
that struts the stage

Of art's parade

In the glare
of darkness,

Until question
illuminates

What art is for

Before creation's
urge
is exhausted

And is denied
the rewards of art

While they deny
the awards of art.

§§§

EPILOGUE

What of art
that never was

Is not of art
that is to come,

When artist
finds it.

*Concealed by choice
or accident,*

Or sterile pride

*That withholds
much longer
than it should.*

*And may never
let go*

*Until risk of fear
overwhelms*

Fear of risk

*That decides
duration's chances,*

*Which equals
that of art,*

*And relies upon
memory*

To exceed it.

*Is it better
to have been,
or not?*

*To ambush time
untimely,*

Or not at all?

*And suffer art's
greatest penalty,*

*When artist
is not the first*

*To be known
for the work.*

But who compels
conscious imprint
of new art?

Does identity
not emerge

While perception
engages spirit
for its tutor?

Still, who knows where
art comes from?

And who knows where
spirit is born?

Even art does not
know itself

Before spirit does.

What of art
that never was

Is not of art
that has arrived,

When spirit
claims it?

§§§

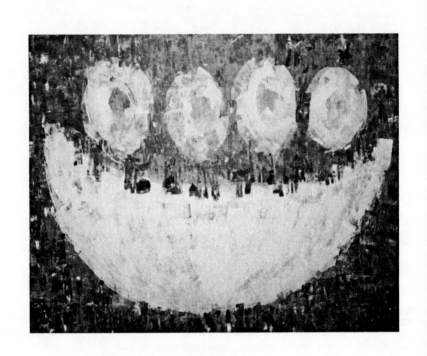

ART

OF

ART

IV

POSTSCRIPT

My art runs two courses: painting and poetry. I alternate between them regularly. They tend to express broad, rather than limited, concepts. The painting is abstract; the poetry universal, and about art. I try to state the timeless in art, to avoid limitations found in an immediate view of it and to allow the widest speculation about it.

I like to feel I am working with what I have not seen in art before, both in style and effect. I must reach beyond what I fully grasp of art to feel I am properly part of it. I think of art as the taste of taste that takes it past its place.

The manner of presentation must reflect my unique technique. Some of my painting exhibits include constructs which have occupied much interior space, as well as gallery walls. That allows me to involve viewers more directly in the art. It is also my aim with poetry, which is not focused upon my personal encounters, but has designs on surrounding everyone's grasp.

My poetry attempts to offer insights as to what art is as it explores the bases and relationships of various art forms. Poetry about art can both focus and expand imagination, for poetry, by its nature, raises questions. In fact, to question may be the most important reason for art to be. I ask a lot of questions about art; questions for which I usually find no complete answers, and about which I have only more questions.

The placement of words on a page, whether few or many, satisfies as thoughts align with them. The space and the spacing are as much a part of the art of poetry as are strokes in painting. Shades of meaning and other basic variables appear in words just as painted color and its shades do. Other similarities also invite comparison.

What is common to all of art is that each of its parts has something to say. Their voices may be nearly imperceptible, or may be booming. They are a product of their coherent tension, their relations to each other and their world.

A work of art is a cumulative product, even when it has its greatest departure from past creation, especially then. During the creative process the artist senses the unforeseen has occurred. It has emerged from subconscious intuition to find and merge with a rhythm—the rhythm of the work.

The Art of Art explores the many facets of art and examines their character in poetic form, discipline by discipline. Since poetry is art, poetry about various art forms expands thinking about them, adding to their meaning. An inescapable conclusion about relations between art forms is that many of their boundaries are artificial. It is most evident when art forms come together as they do in theatre.

Theatre is actually a construct of all art forms. It imagines them a discrete whole. It focuses viewers where it seeks to lead them. In the process it transcends some reality to bring direction its own reality. It has a way of pushing distractions aside, keeping interferences to a minimum. Successful theatre draws us into itself and we cannot help but succumb to its ambition.

Some of the poetry was written at the event of an artistic stimulus. I composed nearly all of Theatre sitting alone on the stage of a darkened auditorium at a university in Michigan, anticipating an art tour of Europe which included theaters. Sculpture began at the site of an outdoor work. Numerous others (several hundred not of this collection) arrived during brief intermissions from painting, usually written in close proximity with my paintings in process.

I intend this work to appeal to the artist in all of us. It represents emotional involvement with art and more. It attempts to define what art is, but from several directions, since there likely is no definition that fully describes even one person's appreciation of art.

My poems engage art and the human experience in their many approaches and responses to each other. I offer them in the hope they will excite pleasure in all who look for it in art.

Dan Matson

VIENNA